## This book is presented to

_____

With love from

_____

Date

_____

# The BLESSING
## *of a* WIFE'S
## LOVE

IDEALS PUBLICATIONS • NASHVILLE, TENNESSEE

ISBN 0-8249-5886-1

Published by Ideals Publications, a division of Guideposts
535 Metroplex Drive, Suite 250, Nashville, Tennessee 37211
www.idealsbooks.com

Printed and bound in Italy by LEGO

Compiled and edited by Kelly Riley Baugh
Designed by Marisa Calvin
Back cover quote by Lord Byron
Cover photograph by Brand X Pictures/Alamy

1 3 5 7 9 10 8 6 4 2

**ACKNOWLEDGMENTS**

CHAPMAN, STEPHEN CURTIS. "When we got married . . ." as told to Mark Moring, from *Today's Christian*, Jan–Feb
2004. CUTRER, CORRIE. "Moving Violations" from *Marriage Partnership* magazine, 2004. "Secrets of Longevity" from
*CAPPER'S* magazine, March 16, 2004. Used by permission of Ogden Publications Inc. FROST, ROBERT. "The Master
Speed" from *Collected Poems of Robert Frost*. Copyright © 1930 by Henry Holt and Co., © 1936 by Robert Frost.
REAGAN, RONALD. "When we got married . . ." from *Reagan: A Life in Letters*. Copyright © 2003 by the Ronald
Reagan Presidential Foundation. Published by the Free Press, a division of Simon & Schuster Inc. SHERMAN, JAMES.
"A Happy Marriage" from *Newsweek*, Nov. 8, 2004. Every effort has been made to establish ownership of each selec-
tion in this book. The publisher will be pleased to rectify any inadvertent errors or omissions in subsequent editions.

**Photography Credits:** Page 9, age fotostock/SuperStock; pages 10–11, Chad Ehlers/Alamy; page 15, Lisette
Le Bon/SuperStock; pages 16–17, age fotostock/SuperStock; page 23, age fotostock/SuperStock; pages 26–27, age
fotostock/SuperStock; page 28, age fotostock/SuperStock; pages 30–31, MTPA Stock/Masterfile; page 35,
age fotostock/SuperStock; page 43, Chris O'Meally/SuperStock; pages 46–47, age fotostock/SuperStock; page 48,
age fotostock/SuperStock; pages 49–50, age fotostock/SuperStock; page 52, age fotostock/SuperStock; page 55,
Aflo Foto Agency/Alamy; page 58, Martin Heavy/Alamy; page 60, age fotostock/SuperStock.

HE FELT NOW THAT
HE WAS NOT SIMPLY CLOSE
TO HER, BUT THAT HE
DID NOT KNOW WHERE
HE ENDED AND SHE BEGAN.

—LEO TOLSTOY

A Wife's
Love . . .
*sweetens*

*A man without a wife is
like a vase without flowers.*

—AFRICAN PROVERB

*The relationship between husband and wife
should be one of closest friends.*

—B. R. AMBEDKAR

# A HAPPY MARRIAGE

*James Sherman*

Linnea and I are partners. We recognize and celebrate our differences as a man and a woman, but we have moved beyond the traditional roles of wife and husband.

My involvement in my children's lives and in the home does not come out of some sense of "doing my share." I'm grateful for every moment I have with them. I consider it my opportunity to be a fully evolved person. When the women's movement allowed women to break free of the conventional, it created the same possibilities for men too. Isn't that, truly, what equality means?

My wife and I are individuals, but we have blended our lives together to create something that's bigger than either one of us.

In practical matters, this means acknowledging each other's strengths. She helps the children with math homework. I help them with English and social studies. I'm a morning person, so I get the boys up and off to school. She's a night person, so she reads to them and puts them to bed. I cook, she does the dishes. I drive, she navigates. Sometimes I pick the movie. Sometimes she picks the movie.

You have to be in love with the idea of being married. This means that you and your partner will be a team. And the team is more important than its individual players.

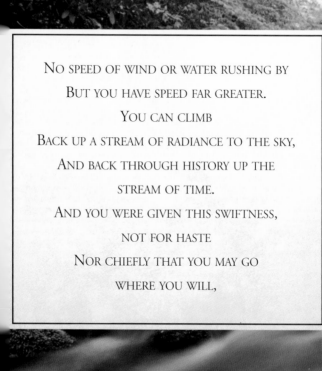

No speed of wind or water rushing by
But you have speed far greater.
You can climb
Back up a stream of radiance to the sky,
And back through history up the
stream of time.
And you were given this swiftness,
not for haste
Nor chiefly that you may go
where you will,

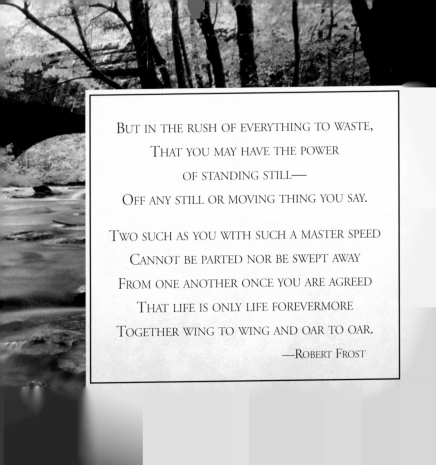

BUT IN THE RUSH OF EVERYTHING TO WASTE,
THAT YOU MAY HAVE THE POWER
OF STANDING STILL—
OFF ANY STILL OR MOVING THING YOU SAY.

TWO SUCH AS YOU WITH SUCH A MASTER SPEED
CANNOT BE PARTED NOR BE SWEPT AWAY
FROM ONE ANOTHER ONCE YOU ARE AGREED
THAT LIFE IS ONLY LIFE FOREVERMORE
TOGETHER WING TO WING AND OAR TO OAR.

—ROBERT FROST

*The world well tried—the sweetest thing in life*
*is the unclouded welcome of a wife.*

—N. P. WILLIS

*Love is the thing that enables a woman to sing*
*while she mops up the floor after her husband has*
*walked across it in his barn boots.*

—HOOSIER FARMER

# A WIFE'S LOVE . . .

## *inspires*

Love is, above all, the gift of oneself.

—Jean Anouilh

At the touch of love, everyone becomes a poet.

—Plato

# SMALL COMFORTS, BIG IMPACT

*Marion Bond West*

When I married Gene after both of our spouses had died, what I wanted most was to be a good minister's wife. His first wife, Phyllis, had been perfect at the task.

My biggest challenge came when Gene took an interim pastorate in Perry, Oklahoma. As we drove there, I struggled with unspoken feelings of deep inadequacy.

That summer morning we were leaving a motel in Jackson, Tennessee, after visiting family in Georgia. Gene was preoccupied with loading the car and planning our day's drive. I picked up the Gideon Bible as I waited for him and prayed for guidance.

"Let's go," Gene finally announced, bags in hand. I started to replace the Bible on the table, then received an unmistakable urge: *Leave it on the unmade bed—open.* I'd never done such a thing before. Yet somehow it felt right, almost familiar.

I left the motel room ahead of Gene, with some hand luggage. When Gene joined me, I was startled to see tears in his eyes. He was so moved he couldn't speak. We both sat silent in the car for a moment, then he said, "That's something Phyllis did in every motel we ever stayed in, as a witness to whoever cleaned the room."

As we headed west on Interstate 40, I felt just a little bit like a minister's wife.

I LOVE YOU FOR WHAT YOU ARE,

BUT I LOVE YOU

YET MORE FOR WHAT YOU

ARE GOING TO BE.

I LOVE YOU NOT SO MUCH

FOR YOUR REALITIES

AS FOR YOUR IDEALS.

I PRAY FOR YOUR DESIRES

THAT THEY MAY BE GREAT,

RATHER THAN FOR YOUR

SATISFACTIONS,

WHICH MAY BE SO

HAZARDOUSLY LITTLE.

YOU ARE GOING FORWARD

TOWARD SOMETHING GREAT.

I AM ON THE WAY WITH YOU,

AND THEREFORE I LOVE YOU.

—CARL SANDBURG

*Her children arise up and call her blessed;*
*her husband also, and he praiseth her.*

—Proverbs 31:28

*Love is a canvas furnished by nature and*
*embroidered by imagination.*

—Voltaire

A WIFE'S
LOVE . . .

*comforts*

*Love comforteth like sunshine after the rain.*

—WILLIAM SHAKESPEARE

*Love seeketh not itself to please,*
*Nor for itself hath any care,*
*But for another gives its ease,*
*And builds a heaven in hell's despair.*

—WILLIAM BLAKE

# MOVING VIOLATIONS

*Corrie Cutrer*

*I can't believe this is happening,* I thought. *I can't believe I agreed to this move!*

Weeks earlier my husband, Bobby, had been offered a great promotion with his company, something he'd worked three years toward. But it required moving. Bobby was excited about the opportunity, and I knew I needed to support him. So I resigned from my job and started making plans to move.

I thought I could handle the change, until I saw the cornstalks—completely opposite of Chicago's skyline.

"Clearly you've made a mistake," I told Bobby. "There's no way we can move here!"

Bobby slumped on the hotel bed. "I had no idea this would cause you so much pain," he said quietly.

I wanted to leave the town and never turn back. Instead, I settled for getting out of the room. I threw on my running clothes and headed outside.

As I ran, I remembered a season of change that had occurred for Bobby several years earlier when he left his job, friends, and family in Tennessee to move to Chicago, where I'd landed a job. He gave up the life he'd established so we could end our long-distance dating. It was my dream of writing that had led us to Chicago. He supported that dream—and me—by packing up and going to an unfamiliar place.

Back at the hotel after my run, I opened the door and apologized for losing my temper. "I'd rather be here with you than in Chicago by myself," I told Bobby. "You are where my home is."

There's a big difference between moving somewhere when you're single and moving somewhere together as a couple. The dynamics are more complicated, and the risks greater.

I have a feeling this won't be the last time we move—or face an unexpected situation in our marriage. But I know that whatever comes, we've achieved a deeper commitment to each other in facing the future together.

*A man reserves his true*
*and deepest love*
*not for the species of woman*
*in whose company he finds himself*
*electrified and enkindled,*
*but for that one in whose company*
*he may feel tenderly drowsy.*

—George Jean Nathan

A WIFE'S
LOVE . . .

*encourages*

Marriage is not just
spiritual communion
and passionate embraces;
marriage is also three meals a day,
sharing the workload,
and remembering to carry out the trash.

—Dr. Joyce Brothers

# BRINGING OUT THE BEST

*Steven Curtis Chapman, as told to Mark Moring*

When we got married, I was clueless. But I soon found out that the only person I was really good at loving was myself. All of a sudden I had all these opportunities to actually live out the truths of Scripture—dying to self, taking up the cross, living for another person. It's so much harder than either Mary Beth or I ever imagined.

But that's what makes it so rewarding. We're both seeing the person God intended each of us to be, slowly coming to the surface. No one else in the world could have ever found all those buttons to push in me, revealing what God

really sees when he looks at my heart. But I also realize there's no other person who could bring to the surface what I've become as a husband and father and a servant of Christ. And, prayerfully, I'm bringing those things to the surface in her too.

We certainly have our differences, but we love each other dearly, and God teaches us through our struggles. To reach over and hold Mary Beth's hand as we drive along, without saying a word, knowing the flames and the floods we've walked through together, is incredible.

Oh, the comfort, the inexpressible comfort of feeling safe with a person, having neither to weigh thoughts nor measure words, but pouring them all out, just as they are, chaff and grain together, certain that a faithful hand will take and sift them, keep what is worth keeping, and with a breath of kindness blow the rest away.

—DINAH MARIA MULOCK CRAIK

It does take quite a man to remain attractive and to be loved by a woman who has heard him snore, seen him unshaven, tended him while he was sick, and washed his dirty underwear. Do that and keep her still feeling a warm glow, and you will know some very beautiful music.

—RONALD REAGAN,
FROM A LETTER
TO HIS SON MICHAEL

The real act of marriage
takes place in the heart. . . .
It's a choice you make,
not just on your wedding day,
but over and over again;
and that choice is reflected in the way
you treat your husband or wife.

—BARBARA DE ANGELIS

A WIFE'S
LOVE . . .

*endures*

True love stories never have endings.

—RICHARD BACH

Teacher, tender comrade, wife,
A fellow-farer true through life.

—ROBERT LOUIS STEVENSON

# SECRETS OF LONGEVITY

*from CAPPER'S magazine*

I've noticed three things about you," a friend said recently to my husband and me. "You respect each other. You not only love each other, you really like each other. And to top it off, you are friends to each other."

When we were first married almost fifty years ago, we tried to be careful to speak politely to each other, to say, "please" and "thank you," and to continue the sweetheart relationship we had enjoyed before our wedding. We decided that our honeymoon need not end just because a baby and other responsibilities came along.

Through the years, we made a practice of observing people whose marriages we admired. We wanted to learn why some couples were so happy.

An eighty-year-old farmer confided to us once, "I have never seen my wife in a dirty dress."

She raised six children, did gardening and canning, cared for chickens, and performed many other duties as a farm wife. They didn't often have people drop in, but if her dress got soiled, she changed to another. She wanted to look nice just for her husband.

A young couple that we've known for many years agreed that he should go to college while she worked in an office. He juggled hours of childcare and study, and she made every effort to keep their small home tidy. They loved and liked each other enough to endure a stressful schedule for several years.

A couple in our church resolved to build a home without going into debt. They lived in a small camper on their land. It took them two years to build a nice home and stay debt-free. It was surely stressful to keep house in such cramped quarters and to homeschool their two children during the long months of building. They were able to endure the difficulties because they are friends to each other.

Observing other couples and learning from them has enriched our marriage.

I shall not greatly care if nevermore
The ships return that I sent out to sea,
Or fortune frowns and bars her iron door
If your sustaining love remains with me.

—CLYDE EDWIN TUCK

We have lived and loved together
Through many changing years;
We have shared each other's gladness
And wept each other's tears;
I have known ne'er a sorrow
That was long unsoothed by thee;
For thy smiles can make a summer
Where darkness else would be.

—Charles Jefferys